NATURE
DEVOTIONAL

NATURE
DEVOTIONAL

ECO-SPIRITUAL
REFLECTIONS, MEDITATIONS

AND

AFFIRMATIONS

REBECCA REITZ

Leaping Hare Press

Introduction

As a child, I took note of the seasons almost more than anything else around me: the sounds, smells, tastes, and feelings. In the dead of winter, even while snow and ice were forming on the blank forest outside my Chicago home, I'd close my eyes and imagine what it was like to bite into a grape, and to have warm sun kissing my cheek and soft grass underneath me.

I remember so vividly trying to communicate these sensations to friends and to my parents, wondering if I was addicted to nostalgia, or if it was simply an appreciation and love for each season's delights and intensities. It's no wonder I made my way into the metaphysical world shortly after heading to college, exploring themes of awareness while working for a company that creates products to put us in tune with the cycles of the moon and sky. And I dove into yoga, reiki, and all the New Age and Old Age practices of that kind.

But when the wellness industry boomed, my social media feed became consumed by daily bio-hacks and people offering schemes to make millions of dollars with manifestation. The overwhelm of the pandemic and the years that followed, have often weighed and riled up my nervous system. I went through a phase of sloughing off practices that no longer felt aligned in an attempt to rebalance with my humanity.

Many practices I kept in my toolbox, and I don't deny the power they hold. But I found that in the most stressful moments, the ones where you feel like you might break—the Earth is the most massive ally and friend you can turn to. Through her seasons, weather, air, and decoration—I feel her say "It's OK; it'll be over soon," or "Here's a sign of change," or "Wasn't today so lovely?"

When I was taught about electricity in my high school physics class, I discovered the concept of grounding. In my adult life, I've learned plenty of meditations and visualizations about sending your energy back into the earth to be recycled. When there is no one else to lean on—not a partner, not a family member, not a pet, not a job—and you feel you can't hold yourself up any longer, the Earth will carry you.

So I take note of when she's bright or dim, growing or taking pause, intensifying or softening. She is the best reminder that we are the Universe, and it is us. We are fire, water, air, stars, trees, leaves, roots.

We're intricate beings and the Earth is like our complicated best friend, along for the same ride. But she knows it well. I'm endlessly grateful for the camaraderie and friendship I've found among the flowers, mushrooms, mountains, rivers, sunsets, clouds.

This book is simply
my own thank you note,
my own journey, my own
friendship with this place
we all call home.
I hope you have your own
story with her that you can
celebrate as well.

1

Early Spring: Quiet Growth

Early Spring

Tastes like
* Warm lentils, bitter greens, biting spices, and cleansing hydrating vegetables

Smells like
* Fresh flowers, dew-covered lawns, fresh linens, and the petrichor of a post-afternoon rain

Feels like
* Dirt on your hands, the cool sweat during a brisk morning run, blankets on your legs as you eat your first meal in the backyard, mud stuck to your shoes, the warmth of a hot shower after being stuck in the rain

* Smiling as you see flowers pop out from underneath the snow

* Happily watching butterfly flutter through a yard

* Neighbors laughing as they eat dinner in the backyard

* Biking as fast as you can to get home before the storm starts

* Wondering if you should wear a rain jacket, or just bring an umbrella, or all the above

* Venturing to the first farmer's market of the season, pining for fresh produce to offset the comfort meals of the winter

* Clearing out the leaves and debris hidden beneath the blankets of snow covering up autumn's smattering

* Unveiling and clearing

* Upheaval, renewal, new beginnings, hope, and the transition towards lightness

Rubber Plant

Reflection

It's a Monday. The sky is overcast and the air is warm.
I walk into my studio space, unpack my lunch into
the fridge and set my computer on my desk. I say
hello to my plants and check to see how they fared
over the weekend. I notice that my small rubber plant
has unfurled a bright burgundy sheath to show off a
new leaf.

This particular plant has traveled with me a lot lately.
Over the winter months, a few leaves suffered from
cold burns. But as this new leaf emerges, I admire the
color gradient: burned leaves at the bottom, spotted
with yellow dots and brown crunchy ends, healthy
greens happily sitting in the middle, and this tiny new
red leaf popping from the top. This contrast is one
I know well at this season of my own life.

I'm currently facing decisions that initially shocked
my system. Aspects of me that were seemingly part of
my healthy façade now mark me. My relationships are
still happy, my routines are thriving, my work is still
flourishing, but certain pieces appear charred by change.
However, that one small leaf I noticed today was a
reminder that growth is happening, hope is to be had,
change births newness.

And below the surface
new pieces are emerging.

Meditation

Close your eyes and focus on your breath. When you are ready, send awareness to each part of your body. Starting with the toes, moving up the legs, through the knees, up to your pelvis, stomach, ribcage, through your fingers, up your arms to the back of your shoulders, into the heart, and eventually up and through the crown of your head.

Notice each sensation. Recognize what parts of your feel on edge, dampened, shocked. Which parts feel comfortable and relaxed. And which parts feel restless or excited.

Move through it all,
breathe through each
uncomfortable sensation,
knowing each part
makes the whole.

I unfold my leaves and
reveal my beauty despite
my sense of readiness.

I unfold my leaves
and uncover my beauty.

I unfold the leaves
I've been working to create and
show the world my beauty.

I prepare in the cold to
bloom in the warmth.

✳

Snowdrops

Reflection

A morning walk is among life's simplest rituals and joys. I take a moment to smell the fresh air, enjoy a cup of espresso, and indulge in soothing my senses before the responsibilities of the day roll over me.

It is early spring, and a blanket of frost or snow covers the yards, cars, and plants. Nonetheless, a few flowers challenge the harsh circumstances. They bravely initiate the transition into spring. Snowdrops, crocuses, and glory-of-the-snows vividly stand out against the backdrop of browns and greys.

Signaling a change.

I sense the same readiness for change within myself. While my appreciation for winter runs deep, I too want to peer out and say "Hello." I might call a friend, start something new, feel warmer air against my skin, and alter my inner rhythm.

There are two sides to early spring: excitement and anxiety. Yet these snowmelt flowers say: "Aren't you excited to see me? We've resiliently made our way through winter! Look! The Earth is ready to play!"

Don't forget that the same holds true for you.

Meditation

*Visualize a version of you
that is yet to emerge.*

What are you wearing?

Where are you traveling?

Whom are you seeing?

What are you working on?

What activities are you drawn to?

*What have you gained after
a season of more solitude?*

What
have you
been yearning
for as we
move from
the stillness
into a
new space?

In the midst
of comfort,
I can step
courageously
into
new life.

❋

Birdsong

One of the truest signs of spring seems to be the first
chirps of the birds. The sound ever-clear as it passes
through the silence of winter. It awakens our sense of
sound, signaling life after the chilling last days of winter.
A cue that warmth and light are near.

Reflection

I attempt to remember the different calls and chirps. Is it a chickadee? A robin? A swallow? A finch? Birds begin their song when they sense daylight, which varies depending on the species. Some start to sing an hour before sunrise, some 20 minutes before. It all comes together to create the notes and crescendos of their early-morning choir, often called the "dawn chorus."

The quiet of the morning makes it easier for males to attract females and flock with their song. The sound is more distinct without the interference of daytime clatter and noise pollution.

Spring intensifies the musical, as it's mating season. Males make an even greater effort during spring to sing louder and clearer to attract as many females as possible and to ward off the competition. However, not all birdsong is sung for mating. Sometimes birds awaken before they can hunt, so they start their song early and stay put until it's safe to head out into the open.

According to writer Jeff Goins, birds sing just before dawn in order to tell their mates that they made it through the night, as a way of saying, "I'm still here." Maybe that's why we sing, too, why we create art— as a way of saying, "I made it. I'm still here."

So as I listen to the peeps and chirps, watching the birds bounce from branch to branch outside the window, admiring their playful and valiant effort to use their voice as a gesture of cheerful togetherness.

Meditation

Close your eyes or take a moment in nature to quiet your mind. Visualize the pops of color and bustling energy of the birds outside. Think of the sounds you hear when you wake. Whether it's the sound of a nightingale, the robin, the mourning dove—try to hear it.

As the sounds layer, can you find your own song within it? What do you want to share after awakening from your winter and nocturnal slumber?

What have you been meditating on, thinking about, dreaming of doing as we transition? Perhaps you're still waking up, and your song feels quiet, or comes a bit later than the others.

Perhaps you woke up earlier than everyone else, ready to loudly call out what you're ready for. Either side of that spectrum is OK. Know that even in nature the birds all sing and call at different times and decibels. Each bird providing its own set of notes to the morning musical.

You are equally a part of that. The world needs your voice as well, how will you remind others that you're still here?

My song is
collectively heard,
loved, and accepted.

I use my voice
to advocate for others
to find my community
to advocate for myself
and to create art
with my words.

✳

2

Late Spring: Blossoming

Late Spring

Tastes like

* Avocados, burrata and apricots, deviled eggs, sweet and peppery radishes and turnips, fresh-caught fish, Swiss chard, strawberries, and beets—pops of reds coloring our bright and crunchy greens

Smells like

* Honey, the plants awakening, pollen tickling our noses, fresh mulch, citrus, and jasmine

Feels like

* A soft bed of grass, cool breeze, and warm sunlight on your skin

* Thickness in the air

* Ducklings waddling behind their mothers

* The exciting burst of a creek awakening the life inside it

* Making wishes on dandelions

* Watching hummingbirds visit the feeder

* Cutting fresh tulips for the dining table centerpiece

* Sitting in awe of the arc of a rainbow

* Shooing and cooing at rabbits in the yard

* Warm and humid air activating our senses

* The familiar buzz of renewal surrounding us

Bald Eagle

It had been a rough night. Our camping trip along the Colorado River had been beset with troubles, with the party being separated on opposite banks by unexpected gale-force winds. But the morning after the storm, a bald eagle soared above our camp: a signal of overcoming a challenging moment. It felt as though it was saying "You made it—with as much poise and humanity as possible, and you'll reunite soon."

Reflection

After the two groups were reunited, another bald eagle made an appearance. We were all huddled on our boats, covering the children with blankets to protect them from further winds and splashes of icy cold water. Looking up at the sky—with wet clothes, cold feet, and fingers, hungry bellies, and low morale—we basked in the beacon of hope this creature represented. The bald eagle is a sign of making it past your edge, a reminder of your capabilities among life's highest pressures. When your courage and wit and strength are tested, and you make it through? That's the energy the eagle brings. How fitting, as usual.

I think of the days leading up to the trip. My partner and I sprinted through another busy week of work, only seeing what was right in front of us, with our daily responsibilities rattling in our heads, naive to nature's potent forces. Forgetting that we've made it through another season barred with COVID-19 restrictions that separate us from our community and our families. Or forgetting that we've created, we've completed projects, we've checked off tasks, we've taken care of ourselves, amid a swirl of heavy world news and personal woes.

The eagle reminds me that spring is a mark of completion and a beckoning to release. Recognize, learn, and move forward. You now have greater perception and wisdom than you had previously. Remember to acknowledge it.

Meditation

*Look to your inner wells
of strength.*

*List the obstacles you've waded through,
the hard times you've navigated, and pat
yourself on the back for making it through.*

Spend time recalibrating your body.

*Release fear, knowing that it
was there for protection.*

*Release pain, knowing that
it was real and part
of the process.*

Recognize
your
tenacity.
Celebrate
your
spirit.

I uncover my power
through challenges.

I radiate strength.

I am resilient.

✳

Mud

An element that seems most present in the spring
is mud. Messy, wet dirt. It sticks to our clean shoes,
splatters onto our cars, and stains the knees of kids'
jeans. It makes a hike or walk a task, and a mudslide
can be detrimental to anything in its path.

Reflection

And while the slimy mixture can be a minor inconvenience to our day, it's an element I have come to respect for its duality. Both animals and humans have used mud to build shelter and soak in nutrients. Mud baths were popular long before modern-day spas were created. The anti-inflammatory properties and number of minerals in mud can relieve muscle pain and calm skin conditions. Mud contains bacteria and microbes in the soil that stimulate serotonin production. It can even lift our mood!

A dynamic force, mud creates fertile ground for us to build on. Although it can feel messy, making things that were once easy to walk on feel like sludge, it ultimately contains the nutrients and minerals needed for new growth. It can be hardened to build things with.

I often think about the concept when things feel mucky in my own life. Especially during transitional seasons like spring or fall, when snow runoff, rain, colder temperatures that thaw during daytime make mud more present around me. I'm in the "muck" as we speak. Feeling self-doubt creep in, burn-out, the exhaustive list of life taking over. But whenever I'm in this headspace, I try to embrace it. Sometimes you just have to accept that you're in the dirt, and things are messy, but it's all to build anew or to restore what you didn't realize you needed.

Think back to a time when you felt like you were admitting a time of muck. A time where perhaps the path was clear, but it felt like it took eons to get to where you needed to go. A time where you had to keep going trudging through each slide backward, maybe even falling here and there. Can you recognize this as a time of growth?

What part of your life needs some calming down?

Now think to where you are now. Imagine you're playing with the mud instead. Whether you're at the pottery wheel throwing clay, building something with it, placing seeds in it, or simply rolling around in it. What are you building, what are you healing? If you're building—what do you want to take new shape or new form? If you're allowing it to heal you—what wounds can it soothe?

Perhaps you feel like you're playing in the mud instead.

I am messy, I am healing,
I am ready to grow.

I embrace the messiness of being
human, knowing that is here to
heal me and help me grow.

I embrace the balance of earth
and water, allowing the water to
heal and rejuvenate and the earth
to reform and rebuild.

❉

Hummingbird

It's nearing the end of April, and I decide to head to the mountains. Finding a nice quiet place to withdraw for a few days. I pack up all of my favorite things—tarot cards, my favorite books, my journal, backpack—and head to Salida, Colorado.

Reflection

I miss winter. I miss being able to say no with more ease, easily blaming the snow or cold for canceled plans or trips. Daylight stretches into our days and everyone is starting to emerge. My extroverted, high-energy partner further contrasting my need to repose.

A beautiful small cabin, with only the things I need— showers and bathrooms in a bunkhouse nearby. A hiking trail around the property. I breathe. I feel. I pause. Feeling the sweetest sense of relief as I check in with my own body, mind, and spirit, and recalibrate it with the helping hand of nature around me. I'm sitting outside basking in the quiet sounds, and a simple book in hand when a hummingbird makes its way in front of my nose. The hummingbird is such a sweet character. Moving so quickly yet seemingly not moving at all. Effortlessly suspended in the air.

After we say goodbye, I decide to consult with the animal medicine deck I brought along.

Of course, the first card I pull is the Hummingbird. The universe makes it clear when it's trying to communicate with me. I laugh at the relevance. But also, a joy runs through me. An appreciation for my call to fertilize the creative seeds I'm ready to plant.

I thank the universe for the sweet medicine. I thank myself for slowing down to see it, even if I too am moving fast. There is magic to be experienced along the way.

Meditation

Allow the hummingbird's medicine to run through you. It floats free of time, tasting the sweet nectar of life's flowers. Remember to embrace the lightness of your being. Instead of feeling tired from darting from one thing to the next, welcome the thought that you are gliding instead. Lift your spirit by appreciating the change in direction rather than feeling overwhelmed by it.

Think of all the things in your life right now. What is your nectar? What are the flowers you find nourishment from? Even the things that feel like responsibilities—can you find the sweetness in them? Now imagine yourself as the hummingbird. How do you currently move from one thing to the next? How can you find positivity in those movements? Excited about what each flower brings?

When you can
recognize the beauty,
gratitude will overflow.
It's in this space that
sprightliness and graceful
agility are achieved.

I embrace the
richness of life.

I choose to celebrate
my delicate grace.

I sip the sweet nectar
of joy, love, beauty that
surrounds me.

✳

03
Summer:
Emergence

Summer

Tastes like
* Sweet fruit, charred vegetables, fresh salads,
and light herbs

Smells like
* Chlorine, salt water, sunscreen, fresh-cut grass,
burning charcoal from the grill

Sounds like
* Distant laughter from the open windows next door
as people gather

Feels like
* Sticky hands from melting ice cream, sweat, a cool
shock of cold from a pool after you have baked in the
sun, the hot-cold sweat after an evening run, the relief
of a breeze, itches from tall grasses and mosquito bites,
aloe vera relieving warm skin

* Napping while sitting in the late-afternoon sun

* Lying on a blanket in the grass watching the sun hang slowly

* Watering the plants with the hose—and then giving yourself a little spritz while you're at it

* Strolling through a market buying fresh produce and pastries

* Long drives with the windows down, blasting music

* The sweet essence of our inner child, playfulness, and joy

* Sinking your toes into the sand

Light
and Warmth

Reflection

We are only a few days away from the Solstice. Amid the daily buzzing of summer—working, traveling for weddings, reunions and celebrations, and meeting up with friends for longer nights, I am recalibrating my schedule to wake up with the sun and go to bed as it sets. As I wake up with it this morning, and honor the few days I have before it starts to slowly fade back to winter—I find gratitude for the brightness, lightness, warmth, joy it brings to us every year. Normally I complain of its heat and its intensity. The altitude of Colorado making it that much more intense. But today I feel the liquid sunshine. I can feel the oozing of light that's seeped into my pores over the last few days of vacation at the beach in Mexico, the days walking in California, and now at home in my daily life. While I normally have to protect myself from it, it's only so I can enjoy it in its full state.

I'm thankful for the bouncy energy it gives.

The inner child work I've felt I can do as I dance in its cornucopia of warmth and light.

Meditation

Imagine the sun's light trickling down
into your body. Through the crown of your
head to the bottom of your toes.

What does it feel like to sit in the sun and
to dip into a pool as it shines down on you?

Feel your system heating and cooling, and
feel its vitality. Feel how much light you can handle,
how much light you can be if you let it in.

Absorb the sun's light into your soul.
"Let's dance," it says. "Let's begin again tomorrow."

You rise and set just as the sun did today.

I dance in the light.

I warm my soul with people
who feel like sunshine.

I know I still glow, even
on a cloudy day.

I illuminate dark.

I cast shadows so I can see
what figure creates it.

I am bright. I am awakened.
I am energizing. I am vital.

❋

Abundance

Coffees in hands. Strollers. Dogs happily walk on leashes. Children latching to the edges of their parents' hands and shirts. Cherries. Local honey. Fresh corn. Towering tomato starters over a happy basil plant. Varities of veggie quiches. Crepes. Tarts. Candles. Baskets. Homemade red sauces, spicy salsas. Mushroom medleys of lion's mane, blue oysters, and maitakes waiting in cartons. Eggs of all colors. Garlic. And of course, bouquets of gorgeous locally grown flowers.

I've been craving them like you crave fresh water after a run. I never do because of their short, sweet life spans. But my crushes on the bouquets take over any sense of self-restraint at this moment. Sea holly's (eryngiums), bright yellow marigolds, blue hues of cornflowers, and pops of small chamomile immediately catch my eye.

Reflection

I gab with my friend as we dart from booth to
booth. Both sipping our iced coffees and teas.
Our bags are happily full of flowers, mushrooms,
and fresh produce. Knowing that's all we should
spend, and also knowing it's exactly what we need,
and no need to take more. We are beaming. Not
because we've never been to a farmer's market
before, but because of how much we missed them
over the past few years. Being there without the
overwhelming fear of catching the infamous
COVID-19 had us shining.

The market reminds me of what I think of when
I hear the word "abundance": community showing
up for each other joyously. Vendors offer us the fruits
of their labor and shoppers honor their gifts with
money in exchange. Conversations, connections,
learning. Everyone filling up on the good stuff.
Feeling like you are with your neighbors, at home,
a place where perhaps we could all take simply care
of each other if we needed to.

As we slow our pace, we make our final stop at the
quiche stand to grab broccoli quiches for breakfast.
As we walk out she turns to me and says "This is just
so lovely. One of my friends said the other day I say
that too much? Do I say that too much?!"

"Not at all," I reply through a laugh, as I know I do the
same. "Things are lovely. And lovely is a lovely word,
so I'm going to keep saying it."

Meditation

Close your eyes and imagine a world where everyone
is celebrated for their gifts, for their offerings: a place
where we all collectively celebrate the harvests of the
earth and the soil that cultivated a rainbow of fruits
and vegetables and herbs; where we honor, give thanks,
and show respect to livestock for the vitamins, minerals,
and protein they provide; where we send praise to the
powdery hands that mixed, kneaded, and baked the
fresh bread and sweet pastries that fill us with joy.

Express gratitude to the hands
that wove the baskets to store
our goods and acknowledge the
reciprocity of people showing up
to support these gifts.

For saying this matters,
I value you.
I value us.

Abundance surrounds me.
Community is where I look for it.
I find joy in nourishment.

Collective care is the essence of love.

I acknowledge simple pleasures
like flowers on the table, fresh
produce on the counter, and a Sunday
stroll to remind myself of the plentiful
wealth we are offered every day.

Our true riches can
be found here.

✳

Fish

"OK, amigos, you're free to dive on in!" Our snorkel guide for the day heartily motioned us to put on our fins and hop off the boat.

My partner and I are both lovers of the water, regardless of our now-mountain roots. Though when was the last time I dove into the open ocean? Had it been years? Not enough time to think through that, or let my fear take me. So I slip my rubbery long fins over my sun-screened feet and put the snorkel over my head. I didn't want to seem afraid, and really, I wasn't. I was excited to reunite with all the beings that live beneath the blue surface.

Like most of us, I can overthink things. What if there's a shark right there? What if I have an asthma attack? What if my flipper falls off? What if I've forgotten how to swim?

Reflection

I dove in.

After fumbling a few times to get my mask clear from
fog and taking a few accidental gulps of salt water,
I found myself in awe of the coral, the schools of fish
moving back and forth with the tide, blue pufferfish
that I actually said hello to, angel fish galore, a seal
sleeping on a rock in the sun, and pelicans diving
towards their food.

I'm cold, but I'm giddy.

Nature in all its various forms puts me back into a
place where I remember I'm greater than my fear.
Look what stepping past it can open up: the existence
of a wonderful, awe-inspiring, mysterious set of
worlds, if you can step past the one thing that often
stops you—yourself.

There are so many times we tip-toe into the ocean
and once we're fully submerged say "Oh, it's not that
bad!" or "Oh wow, it actually feels great once you're
all the way in." And after we dive, we say "Let's do that
again," eagerly excited to feel weightless in the air.
We forget the moments, even these small physical feats,
that remind us the other side is incredible. Or, at the
very least, revitalizing.

Don't think, just dive.

Meditation

*Think of the moments where you've
had to jump. Dive. Swim. Fully submerge
yourself under cool water. Remember your
hesitancy, then remember the decision you
make to push past that hesitancy.*

*Think of the moments in your life,
when you've had to make a choice.
And you made the right one.*

*You found playfulness, joy, relief, and strength,
from pushing past anxiety or fear.*

In releasing fear,
I uncover my own strength.

I trust that spontaneity will
open my curiosity.

I expose myself to find my own
sense of vitality and liveliness.

I release myself into open water,
free to roam, explore, and discover.

I allow my soul to feel
uninhibited by my thoughts.

I let my wild be wild.

❋

4
Early Fall:
Reconnection

Early Fall

Tastes like
* Winter squash and deep-green-collard greens,
apple fritters, dark berries, brown sugar, warmed oats,
the first crock pot of chili or tortilla soup

Smells like
* The smoke of a bonfire, vanilla-scented candles,
pumpkin and apple infused in everything, cinnamon
ciders, leaves decomposing among the fresh crisp air

Sounds like
* Distant laughter from the open windows
next door as people gather

Feels like
* Crunching through leaves, brisk air lightly nipping
at our noses and ears and the warmth of the sun hitting
our cheeks

* The complimentary colors of blue skies peeking through golden leaves

* The inevitable heaviness of the dark and the cold starting to creep in

* Carving pumpkins, making nourishing meals, gathering with people closest to us

* Warmth and cold, dark and light, cloudy and clear, a beautiful dance and harmony among our inner rhythms and nature itself

Hazy Days

Right before fall begins, we experience the relentlessness of summer, when we still see record-breaking heat sneaking into the forecast, when the sun is still high and the final few summer activities come knocking at our door. The kids return to school and "the holidays are just around the corner."

Reflection

This is when the longing for cool air, a cloudy day stuck inside, and a warm nourishing meal grows stronger each day. The promise of shorter days excites the introvert within us all, overshadowing whatever summer plans we may have left. We wish away the summer so quickly when we get to its final days. Our patience is tested, we're overheated, and ready to shift.

I've found that in these final moments of summer I honor the endurance and stamina that got me through the thick heat of summer. That is the moment I am at now. While rest is certainly important, and I certainly daydream of cozy fall days approaching, there's a certain amount of stress that is crucial for my growth. There are blessings to be found in that shaky space.

When I push myself to the edge instead of falling into my comfort zones, I learn how to adapt, and find clarity about what psychologists refer to as the "window of tolerance." In the moments that close summer, I consider the risks I have taken and their rewards. I weigh what awakened me, what felt like "too much", what was fulfilling, how much I can handle happily, what I can integrate more of. It helps me to identify my boundaries. And while it may feel boring in comparison to summer's playful moments, or fall's decorative and cozy offerings, it's in the transition that I find within me the strength to handle life's inevitable unknowns.

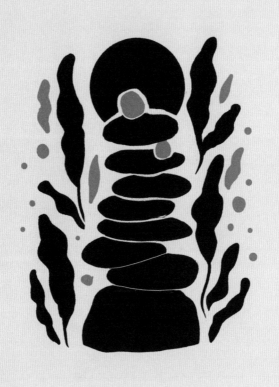

*Look for beauty in discomfort. Your current feelings
of discomfort only illuminate the perspective found
on the other side. Remember how much more refreshing
it is to step in cool water after a scorching hot day.
Remember that extremes are revitalizing.*

*Imagine yourself walking along a shaky tightrope, and sense
the path to balance that this reveals. The need to maintain
strength as you walk this tightrope will guide you to your
center. The things that you endure may remind you of your
ability to support myself. And when you are knocked off
center, you have the opportunity to regather yourself.*

I find courage
when I leave my
comfort zones.

I honor the
perspective that comes
from discomfort.

Life is a dance
of finding comfort and
stepping out of it.

❋

Clouds

Reflection

Clouds are an underrated piece of nature. When we're young, we make out shapes, pointing out the faces, animals, and other things we see within them, in awe of the way they change. They are beautiful pieces of our sky. They pop through our bluebird days like cotton candy, and provide us shelter from the sun, just when it's feeling like too much.

They also carry our rains and snows, and hang low, creating foggy, moody mornings, and paint our sunsets with jaw-dropping colors as they scatter the light and bounce it back towards us.

Clouds that sit in the sky at higher levels intercept more sunlight—sunlight has no color of its own—but refracted through cloud particles, we see the oranges, reds, purples, and blues that make them so spectacular. And while clouds often get a bad rap, there's something about the way they make us feel. At the end of a long day, a vivid sunset gives us pause, fills us with that undeniable sense of awe, the giddy natural high of seeing something so hopeful and joyful.

They can change the course of our day in a minute. Whether an unexpected storm rolls through, or they break up to let some sunshine in, clouds direct the mood of nature.

And what a powerful force that is.

Meditation

Close your eyes. Take a few breaths in and out. As you do so, imagine the various skies you see or have seen. Make a mental image list of the clouds and skies you remember: the rainy skies, the dark skies, the storm-filled skies, the snowy ones, the no-cloud-in-the-sky skies, the sunsets, the clouds that are unfamiliar to your native hometown clouds.

Imagine the times you've been on an airplane, or at high altitude, where you feel like you can nearly touch them yourself. Take a moment to sit with it all.

You have that same energy within you. Clouds are made up of tiny water drops, particles, and ice crystals. You are in charge of your moods as much as the clouds are in charge of the sky's.

Maybe you need a little rain, a little refreshment. Or snow to quiet your soul. Or a sunset to brighten your mood. Or just a plain old cloudy day as a reminder that even nature has its moods: emotional, vibrant, ever-changing, bored, dull, and full of magnificent surprises.

What do you need?
Ask the clouds.

I am a spectrum of cells,
particles, stars, and dust.

I am a masterpiece,
a whirlwind, and dynamic.

Whether I move fast or float.

Whether I block or reflect light.

Whether I am dark
or bright white.

I am not bound to one thing.
I am not afraid to start over.
I let go to make space for renewal.
I nourish new beginnings.
I transform and shift, in accordance
with the clouds, the winds,
and the cycles of my life.

❊

Nesting

The act of making a house a home is described as "nesting." The term is often used in reference to pregnancy, and to women who instinctively start preparing their homes for the arrival of a newborn, but it can simply mean arranging a space: making it feel just right after you've moved into a new spot, or settling into your desk at the start of the work day.

My parents were professional nesters. Even friends of mine that have only been to my childhood home a time or two note their sense of comfort in the space. It was somewhere that always had something bubbling in a Dutch oven on the stove, the smell of food on the smoker outside, warm dimmed lights, candles lit, a football game playing in the background, wine on the countertop, socks just out of the dryer, music playing over the speaker in the family room.

If my childhood home were a season it would be fall. I think fall reminds us that beauty for the sake of beauty is important to us as humans. Our sensory experiences shape our reality, so being in a space that inspires, comforts, makes us feel safe, is so important. To me, fall naturally makes a house feel like a home. It's the time when we reconnect with these spaces and our respect for them.

We look to our homes and our inner worlds to restore us. We take a break between the hustle of summer to the bustle of the holiday season. I think many of us romanticize fall. We love this comfortable in-between space. We take part in appreciating the creature comforts, the earthy world around us, the small things that make a massive difference throughout our day.

We're grateful for the vibrant colors of the trees, the weather going easy on our physical bodies, and the pace of the world seemingly matching our inner rhythms. We get a nice feeling of a time out—where we get to enjoy our spaces, the people around us, and nature with ease.

Meditation

Why not romanticize your life?
Gratitude for the ordinary is an easy
way to access our happiness.

Take a moment to visualize the joys and pleasures
that bring you simple joy. As you do so, make
a mental note to practice this in the moment as well.
The next time you engage in a simple experience
or activity that brings you joy, you can say
"I love this. I'm savoring this moment."

The more you can practice the act of gratitude
in the present, the easier it'll be to savor
every last drop of enjoyment.
Think of it like a bank of positivity.

There is
a goldmine
in the
ordinary.
Feel it,
tell it,
share it.

I find miracles
in the ordinary.

I revel in
day-to-day moments.

I live sweetly
rather than swiftly.

I savor my life like
I savor a good meal.

I make a home out
of my house.

❋

5
Late Fall: Preparation

Late Fall

Tastes like
* Creamed spinach, Brussels sprouts, potatoes, broths, pears, roasted stews, cardamom and pies

Smells like
* Smoked vegetables

Feels like
* Taking a sip of cold air, saying yes to fewer plans

* Cozying up with a pet, covering up with blankets

* Gathering in smaller groups, visiting each other's homes

* Sparking a fire, and lighting candles, allowing the flickering ambiance to relax our systems

* Gold light flooding into the space as a reminder that sunset is nearer than you think

Darkness

The glamor and sparkle of early autumn are beginning to dwindle and the beautiful show of nature has passed. As daylight hours grow shorter, and the air gets cooler we face the fact that our usual routines are about to change if they haven't already. The weather sneaks up on us and shakes our inner rhythm and sense of routine. Everything is suddenly a bit clunkier, a bit tougher to get to.

Many find this time of year detrimental to their mental health and feeling the heaviness of seasonal affective disorder (seasonal depression). Darkness can feel like it closes the curtain on our light.

While it's natural, the problem lies in the pace at which our society moves and the way in which nature moves. Sometimes these can feel painfully in opposition. We sprint to keep up while nature slows down. It's no wonder we experience more colds, stomach bugs and fatigue.

We resist the cycle of the Earth, and to me, it's why we feel heavy. I have experienced dreadful Chicago and Midwest winters for the majority of my life. In these places, no one underestimates the brutality winter can bring. I've learned along the way that the more we resist and resent the changing winter brings, the harder it is to prepare.

For me, late fall can be a beautiful time to reconnect with our physical systems. To ask ourselves what we need rather than follow what it wants. To find joy in smaller moments, stock the house with ingredients for nourishing soups and hot soothing teas. To take longer showers and find ourselves having the first weekend in months without plans.

Meditation

Ultimately, late fall is a time to take a big step back or a big step inward. In slowing down and experiencing darkness, you can find yourselves better prepared for what lies ahead.

Lean into this moment of absolute presence. What are you trying to run from? What lights are you trying to keep on as you navigate your darkness? Allow the darkness to be a cleanse, a restart, a moment to catch your breathe. An energetic sleep.

You already have a glimpse of what is to come. It's crucial to remember how to take care of your systems. What will you need in your toolkit as I enter winter's stage? What new habits and behaviors can you incorporate to find daily joy in the slow down?

It's exploratory. Have fun without distractions, and see what your soul needs as you prepare for the days to come.

This time with yourself is precious.

Darkness

is

essential

to

finding

my

light.

✳

Fox Energy

Last night, I felt like looking to my medicine cards for some inspiration. Even when my mind is crowded and my schedule is busy, they always have the perfect message and and lead me to create personal work. This time, I pulled the Fox card, and as this resonated with me.

Reflection

I love the energy foxes bring during these colder months. It feels like this bouncy, joyful, mystic creature pops in to say: "It doesn't have to be boring just because it's cold!" They're intelligent and clever. Aware of their surroundings, confident about their destination, and able to joyfully prance and leap through the harshness of the cold.

The fox reminds us that our ability to adapt is one of the greatest skills we can possess. When we see obstacles as a challenge, we start to turn on the parts of our brains that want us to succeed. We want to win the game and we're driven by positive results.

When we take time to observe,
to slow down, to listen,
we find the ability to navigate
situations with a bit more ease,
fun, and confidence.

These are hitting home for me and how I feel in my own ecosystem right now. I'm trying to keep sharp, stay eager, remain aware and discerning, in my lane and on my wave. I'm forever thankful for tools like these cards to give me guidance amid a sea of new experiences and lessons to be learned.

When we engage
our inner fox energy,
the easier it is to
navigate the situations
that come our way.

When we are attentive
to the present moment,
we grant ourselves more
peace for the future.

Meditation

*What's that thing, the object that brings you the
most comfort? Something you love. Imagine your
most prized possession. See it in front of you.
Perhaps it's a piece of gold jewelry, a printed
polaroid photo, a paperback book, an old keepsake.
Feel it in your hands. Is it metal, wood, soft and cozy?
Small, large, or awkward in size? Is it something you
can smell? Think of as many characteristics as you can.*

And now imagine that that thing is lost, in a large forest.

*Picture yourself searching for it,
retracing your steps, keeping your eyes open and alert
for any sign of it. Keep moving through the forest.*

*Suddenly, you notice out of the corner of your
eye a brighter color, something that is not natural.
You walk over, and behold. Your beautiful favorite
thing right where you left it.*

Observance keeps me
in tune with the world.

Listening is my portal
into knowledge.

Discernment is a skill
of self-respect.

❋

Mushrooms

The natural world has been stripped down, and the harsh winds leave me feeling raw, like the bark of a tree encountering its first storm. And it is amazingly quiet. Even as an introvert, I forgot how lonely the quiet can make me feel. But while the party upstairs may seem bland, brown, slushy, and bleak, there's more activity below our feet. The party has just moved downstairs, so I consider the hosts of the underground party— the ones that bring everyone together: the fungi.

They are masters of the life–death cycle and no challenge is too fierce for them. We often think of fungi as the fruit-bearing mushrooms visible on the surface, but below ground, we find thin strands called hyphae. These branch into a larger web called mycelium. The mycelium extracts and recycles nutrients in the soil, connecting multiple plants, even ones of different species, allowing them to communicate with each other. In a mutually beneficial exchange, fungi keep the trees healthy and are rewarded with nutrients from photosynthesis.

I find this symbiotic relationship incredible. It is the most powerful reminder that love, giving, and community prevail in the harshest conditions. So as fear of scarcity sets in, or as I mourn for the things I let go of this year, or I find myself sinking into sadness, I am prompted to send a signal; to call a friend; to make a meal for someone going through a hard time or to tell someone that I'm going through a hard time. And, whether I receive in return advice, patience, an unexpected gift, a nice note, a hug ... these moments give me the boost I need within my own vessel, and in turn, I'm happy to do the same for others. Interconnectivity is crucial for our own vitality.

Meditation

Find a time recently when you've felt stuck in one of those "Does anyone else feel this way?" moments. Did you interact with others in a way following those experiences that eased you through them?

Think or write about your own root system: the people have made you feel less alone, whether expected or unexpected. Imagine you are a mushroom, a tree, or even a mountain, and see your root system stretching out below you in a web, flickering with the light from these people.

Whether they gave advice, shared a similar experience, or opened your eyes to a new perspective or opportunity, it's a beautiful thing to watch our own systems vibrating around us.

In the hours that feel most isolating, remind yourself you are not alone. There is a vast network of humans that are inherently happy to help you.

And when you feel that your own cup is full, or your own needs are taken care of, you can provide happily to those around you. The circle of giving and taking this energy, feeding it, and recycling it throughout our own networks, is profoundly healing.

Nurturing the root systems around us only makes us stronger.

I am connected to many
hearts, minds, thoughts,
and perspectives that fertilize
and enhance my own being.

I rediscover my own vitality
when I'm surrounded by the
healing energy of others.

I give my own energy
and resources when I feel
my cup is full.

Taking care of others, and
allowing them to take care me
of me, sends warmth through
every ounce of my being.

✳

6
Winter: Stillness

Winter

Tastes like
* Thick creamy cocoa, persimmons and peppermint, nutmeg and clove, caramel and clementines, toasted bread and steaming soups

Smells like
* Wood burning on the fire, sugar and bread, vanilla-scented candles, pine needles

Sounds like
* Boots crunching into the snow, the slow crack of the fireplace, the silence of the air outside

Feels like
* Cold tipped noses and ears

* Thick robes and slippers, thick snowflakes nesting in your hair

* The melting sensation on your skin during
a steamy shower

* Scraping the sidewalk with a shovel to clear snow

* Bundling into a burrow of blankets, the tranquillity
of stepping outside into quiet

* A richness that reminds us to enjoy the simplest
of things, to celebrate together, to

* Recuperate, to indulge, and to take deep
nourishing care of ourselves, to bask in the quiet,

* To confront the cold, to savor the warmth,
to eat good foods, to enjoy our homes,
to be Grateful

Snowflakes

As we all curl up, hibernate, reflect on the year, and retreat before the arrival of spring, the snow falls around us. We watch the flurries create blankets of white— I wonder how many snowflakes are piled up. As many as the grains of sand on a beach? Or stars in a galaxy?

Reflection

While I don't know the answer, what I do know is that snowflakes are one of those natural wonders when you see one up close.

I don't remember when I first discovered the work of Masaru Emoto—but I remember hearing about his experiments and studies of how the structure of water changes in relation to the sounds, words, and thoughts it's exposed to. Water that was exposed to words denoting love, compliments, peace, and gratitude generated otherworldly, beautiful crystalline patterns when frozen; whereas, words like "evil," and "depression," or even the sound of heavy metal, caused nondescript blob-like ice crystals to form. Regardless of the scientific backing of his work, his images of water crystals and the corresponding sentiments exposed to them, are still fascinating.

As humans roughly 60% of our bodies are made up of water. And while the Moon affects the tides, I also believe the Moon likely has an impact on our physical bodies. So when I saw Dr. Emoto's work, I couldn't help but wonder the same. And every time I see a perfect snowflake fall gently onto my coat, or I watch a storm of snowflakes flurry in the wind, I'm reminded of this idea.

That I am made up of water, and while I may not have a million beautiful symmetrical ice crystals forming in my body, my thought patterns and words have an impact on my physical being.

Watch and feel
yourself swell into
a symphony of
beautiful crystalline
shapes, like intricate
stars glistening
with light.

Meditation

Think of your body as its own version of a snowflake composed of water, as if you can peer inside and see each crystal of water.

Think of what love feels like: receiving a compliment, giving a compliment, a hug, a thoughtful gift or birthday card. Feel it all coming into your body and being soaked into each particle.

Think of what compassion feels like: peace, balance, hope, inspiration, pleasure, joy.

Let these thoughts cool you, inspire you, uplift you. You are a beautiful creation, you can choose beauty within at any moment.

These emotions are not outside of us, they are available for us to access. Pull them in, and let your body drink up all the beauty this world has to offer.

Remind it of the love that it expresses in this physical world. As your body glistens with light, imagine each crystalline droplet moving outward, falling like snowflakes to others you love. Pouring and sprinkling the beauty you have cultivated and spreading it back into the universe.

I am a vehicle for transformation.

I have the ability to create
a snow globe of beauty, inspiration,
love, peace, and serenity inside
my own consciousness.

Everything within me is
an expression of what I choose to
fertilize my physical being with.

I choose to speak to myself
with radical care, restructuring
the energy within, and allowing
beauty to take its form.

✳

Hygge

For as long as I can remember, I've been sensitive to light, especially man-made light. I always felt great relief the moment I'd exit a classroom or office with a flickering fluorescent ceiling light. It was as if the fake brightness were seeping into my skin and riling up my nervous system. My college roommate used to laugh at me for the slew of golden-toned lamps and candles I had in my room. "Can you even see what you're doing?"

Reflection

Sometimes I couldn't. But something about
the candlelight felt like peace and warmth
and ease. Back then, it felt like a small quirk,
but I now have a deeper understanding of this
insatiable need for good ambiance. While we
can appreciate the snow crunching under our
feet, or a brilliantly red cardinal popping into
view against the bland winter landscape, it's
much harder to connect with nature in the
winter months. I'm sure we all dread leaving the
workday only to head home in the dark.

When the Danish term "hygge" gained popularity,
I learned that my obsession with ambiance could
be traced to the need for fire. While I often
visualize fire as a raging volatile thing, I now
also know that it can be the cute little flame of
a candle sitting on your desk. This is the season
when fire truly shines (and we notice it). The other
elements wouldn't be available to us in the winter
without heat. For most of the year, the heat can
feel uncomfortable; but in the winter, it's essential.

Fire keeps us alive—plain and simple. But it also
has a nostalgic emotional quality to it. Whether
it's the fire crackling in the background of a social
gathering, drinking a hot tea from the stove,
or watching the windows fog up, knowing I'm
encased in a bubble of warmth from the cold
outside—I tend to feel immense gratitude and
solace in these moments.

Meditation

Imagine the feeling of the cold hitting your cheeks, stuffing your hands into your armpits, as you walk through snow, skipping around patches of ice as you make your way up to a set of houses.

You see one that looks even more cold. With blacked out windows, a single porch lamp glowing, and the snow in front of the house glistening only from the light of the moon.

Next door, you find a home with lights trailing up to the front, candles clearly lit at the table inside, laughter and music burst from within, and you can feel the heat of light warm your entire body.

The choice is easy.

Luckily for you, this is a simple practice to remind you that warmth can be created in moments big and small.

Rather than visualize warmth, why not create it? If you can, find tea lights or simple pillar candles to adorn your home with light. Spend time allowing the lamps, candles, and reading lamps to give your environment the glow humans have connected to for years.

I invite connection inside.

Love, courage, strength, power.

I connect to others, understanding
that they can stoke my own flames.

I cultivate hospitality in my
community and in my own space.

I fan my flames to show myself
and others that I am here.

❋

Solstice

The Winter Solstice is a sacred moment to honor warmth amid cold, the duality of light and dark.
The day is always a reminder for me to pause and thank myself and all sides of myself. The parts that cool me down when I'm hot, the parts of me that warm me up when I'm chilled. The parts of me that illuminate a path forward when I feel dark, and the parts of me that turn off the lights when it's too bright or I'm overwhelmed.

Reflection

It's the moment where it feels like we can zoom out
a bit, and see all sides of our life with clear eyes. We can
take stock of what is out of balance, what is of value to
us, what we'd like to cultivate, and what we'd like to
graciously let go of. We get our own moment to pause.
And remember how cyclical our own rhythms are as
well. It's a lovely day to reflect.

The Solstice invites us to celebrate our path. Our year
is a story of its own and the Solstice is the final chapter,
the denouement to the narrative, the moment when
we see the plot's resolution, or at the very least unravel
it for good or bad. Traditional rituals and celebrations
around the Winter Solstice involve fire: lighting candles,
gathering around a bonfire, burning the clocks, releasing
lanterns of lights … all honor fire, a necessary element in
the face of winter. Whether you are lighting a new way
forward or burning what no longer serves you—take
this day in all its dual-natured glory.

Look at your past with
grace, honor the present
with gratitude, and light the
fire that will blaze and light
your way into the future.

Meditation

Relax your jaw.

Take a deep breath in.

Move your head in circles.

Listen to your body.

*The sun is coming back to us, so acknowledge
your inner fire by awakening your own body.
Release the tension you've been carrying,
by arching your back like a cat after a long nap.*

*It is not necessary to remain
perfectly in balance.*

I honor the
inhalation as
much as the
exhalation,
and every pause
in between.

✳

Flowers,
trees,
Sun,
and Moon
enjoy this
same process
taking the
changes,
redirects,
and cycles
with faith.

So I release—

Each pebble of heaviness
that is perhaps not mine to carry
is lifted, one by one, into the sky.

A beam of light pushes fearful
thoughts back into the ground,
to the core of the Earth.

Each worry is placed in a basket
to be taken away for a while,
maybe forever.

The ocean's waves pull
grains of sand I no longer
need back into its depth.

Leaping Hare Press

First published in 2023 by Leaping Hare Press
an imprint of Quarto. One Triptych Place,
London SE1 9SH, United Kingdom
T (0)20 7700 6700
www.Quarto.com

A catalogue record for this book is available from the British Library.

ISBN 978-0-7112-8068-7
Ebook ISBN 978-0-7112-8069-4

9 8 7 6 5 4 3 2 1

Commissioned by Monica Perdoni
Edited by Michael Brunström
Designed by Mylène Mozas

Printed in China

Rebecca Reitz is an eco-spirituality advocate and illustrator living in
Denver, Colorado. Through her work with @spiritdaughter and her
personal designs, she aims to inspire others to notice, appreciate, and
respect the spiritual energies, power and patterns of nature, through
the seasons, elements and the divine feminine. You can find her
perpetually inspired by the wildlife and mountains that surround her,
always seeking where the universe may take her next.